Loving All These Heartbreaks For Us   Cathy BLUE

Original Name: Loving All These Heartbreaks For Us
Original Language: English

First edition, July 2021

Book design by Tülay ASLAN
Cover Photo by Tülay ASLAN

ISBN 978-625-00-9816-5

Published by Tülay ASLAN

Index

I have had so many people supporting me to write, all of my life. If anything, I feel grateful.

My biggest thanks go to my amazing, dear twin, *Emily, you should come and share the spotlight, it is so freakin' bright up here! I love you to the moon and back, my soul sister!*

My second biggest thanks goes to my kids, they made me selfless, they taught me the definition to love someone with every fiber of your being, in good and in not-so-good days. *You two are my darling babies, every day, every moment, I'm proud of the people you guys are becoming, I love you guys so, so sooooooooooooooo much!!!!!!!*

To all the other selfless poets and poetess i had met over Instagram, wow, you/we guys are an amazing community there, everyone trying to lift each other, taking their time to read and make comments. You guys have made me feel so welcomed and I can't thank you guys for that! I am sending my best wishes to all of you!

Definitely not the last but to all artists / musicians / writers / painters / photographers...who make people smile, laugh, cry every day without even knowing. You shine brighter than a star!

Cathy

Summer Vibes

Frozen till my bones
In this summer heat.
Miss your warm voice.

Anchored

You are the wrong one for me,
Yet, I am the right one for you.
‘Cos I will stand tall and proud beside you,
Pull you back to your feet,
Every time,
You drag me down.

Minimalist

Writing with less words,
Somehow feels more.

Can an unexpected brush of your lips
Replace the excitement of making-out
While snuggling on the couch?

That smirk and glint in your eyes,
When you understand,
What I am exactly talking about,
Instead of....words.

A sincere hug,
Given without being asked or feeling pressured.

I miss the days,
When you were a minimalist,
Not that automatic programmed robot.

Heartbroken

Of all these simple sentences
Of 3 words,
I truly wish
'You broke me'
Would never be the one
I had to overuse.

Flight

The excitement and fear of the unknown,
Before you jump off a cliff,
Open your wings and fly.

How my life feels nowadays
When I have to stand in front of that cliff,
Debating if it will be my eternal falling
Or a ride of pleasure.

Guard

Press your lips on mine hard,
Suck the life out of me.
My blood will set me free,
From this world,
From your eternal prison.

Star

Have faith in yourself,
All these missing pieces will find their places.
Your fate was planned much more
Brighter than this.

Sand Castles

You were that stubborn wave,
Washing away
All the sand castles I built.

The more I built,
The more you demolished.
Where does it leave us now?

Frigid

Men brag about
Knowing the difference
Between sex and making love.
Clueless they are,
Blind to see,
When your woman has sex with you,
All the time,
Rather than making love,
RIP all her love.

Status Update

One of these nights,
Lying awake in bed,
Watching the ceiling,
Inhale and exhale.

Mind is exploding with self-guilt and shame
For knowing,
I could've handled that better,
I could have been more patient.

Pain throbbing inside my skull.
Just one of those nights.

The Slayer

You stayed floating in the muddy water,
I swam back to the shore.
They called me survivor.

You stayed loyal blindly,
I slayed all these bonds that tried to keep me down.
They called me selfish.

You always muted yourself.
I never bothered to hold my tongue,
They called me sharp-tongue.

You gave up all yourself to please them,
I gave the world my middle finger to keep myself.
Ironic it is, they hated me
But again they did not love you either.

The bottom line is
<u>Do not try to please the freaking world.</u>

Platonic

All these words I gave birth,
Thinking of you.
None of them are read
By you.

Husky

I dream of your husky voice inside my ear,
As you line kisses to my neck
In a parallel universe.

Possibilities

Deep in my my heart I know
We are meant to be together.
I think this will have to wait,
For a parallel universe.

Whoring Around

Many lips you had kissed
For empty promises of hourly pleasure.
In mine, you will find love.

Many skins you had touched
Without any emotional attachments.
World watched you going down,
The emotional baggage you carry
Weighted you down.

Many faces, eyes, you just looked.
Look at my eyes,
Find your way back to yourself
So you can love me more.

Husky 2

Racers by nature,
Rivals by nature,
Can they defeat the fate,
Break the circle,
Fall
In love
With each other?

Religion

I have turned my back to their religions,
Chose the safety of your arms.
Enlighten me,
Lead the way,
I'll follow.

Genie In A Bottle

I want to lay in the bed,
Facing each other,
Legs intervened,
Talking about
A Future
We will have.

Rub me baby, rub me well
Heat me up.
I will make
All your wishes
Come true.

Silent Scream

Silent screams for
It has always been your name
I want to scream out
On top of my lungs
When I come undone.
Never his.

Tripping

Every time I walk down
The aisle of our memories,
It is my guilt trip.

My lips follow the salty taste of your skin,
All the curves and all the glorious scars
As far as it goes down,
Down my guilt trip.

Numbers

One question that still haunts,
What had happened to us?

These five words
That could change the story
I was wrong, Forgive me,
Never left your lips.

Now, eleven miles away
Feels like another parallel universe.

Four pairs of shoes are left
In front of my door.
None of them are yours anymore.

Walking Amongst Wolves

-For Sanora, with all the love of this world-

Run deeper into the woods
The night breeze licks our thick fur.
It is a wild run, we stay alert.

We sniff our prey,
Oh sweet baby deer,
All that brownish fur
Coated in crimson now.

I howl on top of my lungs,
They said "*it does not decrease the pain,*
But at least now, you are heard."

Tell-A-Tale

I

I came, I fought.
You may claim I lost it,
At least I put up a fight.

II

Lowering our guards tonight,
In the promise of no attacks,
We all have dead bodies
To bury
Or burn.

III

Listening to the crackling of the fire,
Warriors, friends that had my back
Are now on their eternal rest.

IV

A swig of an ale,
A bit of salt to the wound,
To remind me everyone
I had loved and lost.

V

Tomorrow,
A new day,
A new chance
In this endless loop
Of self-doubt and self-love.

Swinging

Resentment, anger, frustration, self-loathing, doubt,
guilt,
All bottled up in the hollow of my chest,
Labelled and branded, dusted off.
All sparkly clean sitting neatly on the shelves of my
mind,
With resilience as my undertone.

My untamed demons met my carnally armor,
Tearing me down to pieces, enjoying their last dinner.

You say *I am beautiful*,
If i stripped down my pretense,
There is only hell for angels.

Music

Your music soothes the longing of the soul,
Makes me smile dreamily as i zone off to neverland,
Eternal memories of lovers, all these promises,
Discovering, hungry touches, quick kisses...
I am dreaming of these and much more,
Your voice is a place to call home.

My body is spent yet eager,
Let's go home.

Prize

I want you to claim your prize,
Not a kiss from my lips.

I want you to hear your name
When I whisper it back
In your ear,
My nails marking your smooth skin.

Tranquility

So many thoughts inside my head,
So many voices,
I do not think I can
Find tranquility
In this world,
Until I am
Lowered down
To my eternal beauty sleep.

History

Close the distance between our lips,
The rest is history.

Stargazing into your eyes
Starless, dark blue sky
Everything else...history.

Nightmare

Hugging your cold body for one last time,
Putting it in a small coffin,
Lowering to the ground.
Worst nightmare, in the blink of paranoia.

Hard Lessons

Everything about you is hard,
I've always learnt it the hard way.

Your bruise whenever you love,
Hold too tight and suffocate.
Pull too hard and crash.
I'm not walking on eggshells here,
Rocks, pebbles and gems more likely.

Got bruises and cuts to prove my point.
All under my skin, in too deep.

Fire

-''writing letters addressed to the fire'' is a prompt, from Evermore by Taylor Swift-

Writing letters addressed to the fire,
Eager for the warmth,
It will provide in the embrace of a lover.

Writing letters addressed to the fire,
Watch everything burn and blur
In front of my eyes.

Writing letters addressed to the fire,
It will not write back yet.
It feels less hollow than your touch
When flames lick my skin,
Scorch and brand my skin,
Swallow me whole.

Hunter

Chasing after you,
I can smell your innocence
The darkest fear.

Run baby run,
Your sweet scent lingers in the air,
Makes the chase more intriguing.

Run baby run,
Run for your precious life,
I'll catch you,
I'll have my feast
On your
Cold, little black heart.

Too Much

I knew my love was always
Too much,
Too dark, too twisted,
Too deep,too emotional,
Too good for you.
A shallow skirt-chaser like you
Is always pronounced as *nightmare*.

Felt too much,
Cried too hard.
Ate a little,
Drank it all up.
Now, looking back at the stranger
In the mirror
In my nightmare.

Wanna Stay Sober

I am high, totally intoxicated,
Drunk on promises,
Always forgotten or ignored.
Tried to move on, stop the addiction,
Always fell back to square 1.

Your lips are moving,
Trying to drug me so
You can rape me again.
I was drunk on promises
Tonight, I wanna stay sober.

O

His hands roam around my body,
Touching the pearls on my chest
The lust is immerse,
I rise and shatter,
Spent yet grateful.

Rise And Shine

Glimmers of yellow and orange
Dance inside your eyes
When you lean in to kiss me,
Hands eagerly reaching to cup my face,
Pupils dilated in arousal and anticipation,
Sunshine embraces us,
Thawing the chill of a loveless life
From our bones.

Soul Tiring

I am tired of being tired,
Physically, mentally, emotionally drained,
Like an empty bird nest, hollow.
Watching the ceilings for hours every night,
Because these self-doubts, what ifs,
Endless possibilities and self-guilt
Haunts me down in every breath.
Little peace I feel sometimes
Feels like a leaf in the wind.

I am tired of being tired,
Tired of having to drink it away
To hush hush all the voices in my head
Only for a couple of hours of night sleep.

Kiddos

You, who opened my sun's in my heart,
That innocent smile on your chubby face,
The glints of mischief in your eyes,
Your giggles are music to my soul.
I have never loved anyone
The way I had loved you.
I can melt down the entire universe.
Love, mummy.

Rainy Days

I hurt in silence, like rain
I hid in a corner, lick my wounds clean.
I spoke, they turned deaf,
I wrote, they turnt blind.

I hurt in silence, like rain,
They shrug all my tears off,
Wash their hands clean,
Go home.

Lipstick

You said "*kill or die*",
Pretty sure I was the easy target.
I whistle, smile like a Cheshire cat,
Dipping my middle finger in your blood
Painting a lipstick on my face.

Fragile Ego

They have always painted us
As the fragile flower,
Because they were afraid that
We were strong enough to
Hold a sword in one hand,
A child in other hand,
Still manage to slay
All of them,
Their poor, fragile ego.

Incubus

I am a sinner,
Rising from my grave every night,
Igniting the flames within you.
Inside this cocoon of haze,
Lost inside the passion I create,
All of you want to get high,
Rise and explode
Like fireworks.

Game-Addict

I hear you say
''She is not such a flirt
As she plays out to be''
Darlin', let me fix a misunderstanding here;
It is not that I can't,
-You know, flirt.-
It is that I do not care to do so.
Do tell,
What is a poetess
If she can't dance around and play with words?
I can make you swoon,
I can make you lovesick,
But playing you a fool
Is more like my style.

Choking Hazard

Life is dull until I hear your breathing,
You are the reason for drinking,
Your hypnotizing aura suffocates me,
Fireworks of emotions, I can not breathe.

Wrong Way

Listen mindfully
to the lilting intonations of your pounding heart,
It's trying to remind you of
All the times you mistook attention for interest,
Flirt for love, lust for longing,
Lies for truths, sex for making love.
You are spiraling down
This old endless road again.

Broken Promises

The smile you give me is twisted
With the lies you try to hide,
Hoping to fool me.
You talk, on and off,
Deviceful words for a naive heart.

Been there, done that.
You won't fool me anymore.

Necromancy

My skin feels rotten and damp,
Layer by layer,
It is falling off.
I shred, I self-destruct,
One layer at a time.

My bones feel wobbly,
Not sure how long
Will these jelly legs
Support the load
I have to carry?

Bearer of news
From another dimension,
Reason of your fears,
Do I look that ugly?

You killed me,
Another man found me
Rose me up
From my ashes.

Loving All These Heartbreaks For Us Cathy BLUE

He promised
To love me,
To cherish me,
Till his death
Tears us apart.

Even then he will
Teach me
How to raise him
From his own ashes.

Forever together,
Our rotten bodies
Causing a tangle of
Corpses of
Previously loved ones.

I will love you,
Forever.

Hunteress

I am turning black,
Guzzling down all the light
You left turnt on.

I am growing darker
In each breath you take,
In every kiss you give to others.

I am extending, shattering, crashing together,
I am reaching-*oh*-so very high,
Babe, you have no idea.

My heart has turned cold and black,
Nothing holds me back anymore,
I will haunt you down,
In every breath you attempt to take.

I will swallow you whole,
My little prey,
When the right time comes.

Itchy

I wanted you to be so many things
A passionate lover,
A thoughtful listener,
A real partner to stand by my side.

You had chosen to be an itch,
I tried so hard to resist the itching,
Cos once you start, you never stop.

I dig up my own grave,
When my fingers began to itch.
Now, it turned into an allergy.

I am so high
On the meds they gave me
To make me forget.

Not just you, not just the itch
But me and life itself.

Stardust

The artist painted a pitch black sky,
Angels added hues of blue, purple, navy.
God sighed, added stars for a little light.
The devil smirked and crashed
All the painting and canvas
Into stardust,
Crumpled all around my feet.
I stared down, sighed,
‘‘Oh my God, what a mess
You had done,
Playing the blind!!!!’

Costumes

"What will you wear this year for Halloween?"
You asked out of blue.
"My haunted heart on a sleeve."
I replied, holding your clueless gaze.

Loaded To Fly

In dreams, we enter a world
That's entirely our own.
Away from their judgemental gazes,
From their harsh words,
The unexpected lash outs,
For a couple of hours,
We try to heal,
These fragile wings are
Too loaded to fly.

Me Versus Us

I am digging myself a grave
To love you more,
This fragile human body,
Limited, too shallow
For you and me
At the same time.
Letting go of me,
Losing myself in us.
So we can be
One together,
Zero apart.

Conquest

Like a conquest or a war,
All the things we do
To win the game of two
Called *love.*

Love Spell

Standing naked under the moonlight,
Chanting in a now forgotten language,
I walk inside my sacred circle,
Saying prayer over prayer,
I offer my blessings, gratitude,
Yet, always ask for more.

The night breeze licks my skin,
I cast a spell on you,
I tie you down by love,
I watch you tug,
Shackle the chains of love.
It makes me cackle with joy.
My wolves howl in agreement.

Enchantress is my name,
I am the master of
Dolls, puppets and more.
Try you may to survive,
A slave is all you will be,
Never a survivor.

Butterfly

You had always been the boy
Ripping the wings of butterflies
For your sheer pleasure.

I was always naive to believe
By letting you rip my wings,
May be another pair
Would grow instead,
Far more dazzling,
Breath-taking.

But again,
You had never been
The type to appreciate
The Beauty
Without destruction.

Light Me Up

I wanna be the lightening
That lights up
Your pitch black starless sky,
When you come undone.

Liar, Liar, Panties On Fire!

I wrote down all the memories of us,
I could remember.
I put them in a time capsule,
Buried under the pile of your clothes.
I lit a cigarette, set them all on fire.

Now, no-one knows
About us.
I guess I will not be
Your dirty little secret anymore.

Pit-Y

''Chin up girl,
You get this,''
I keep saying to myself.

Your voice still
Catches me off guard
Whenever my playlist shuffles.
I fall back to the bottomless pit
All over again.

Self-Growth

I found my voice,
I found myself.
I found my inner strength,
Embraced the restless warrior I am,
Back off the world,
The more I am growing,
The louder it will get.

I ain't gonna play
Your muted dull puppet
Any more.

Stain

Drunk on the sweet release,
Disgusted in my weakness,
I cry, sitting in the cold bathtub.
I wash you off my skin,
It leaves bruises and stains.

Fate

They sat down in their thrones,
Looked down to us.
One of them turned and said,
"I can't read her fate,
Your handwriting is impossible
To read."
Another one laughed,
Waving an impatient hand, she said,
"Go with what you think it is then."

Whiskey Dreams

Watching you over my whiskey glass,
I undress you silently inside my head,
Your black t-shirt goes first,
Oh boy, oh boy,
I definitely like what I see.
I lick my lips, imaging yours on mine,
My hands itch to rip those jeans off.
I take a sip of my whiskey,
Feel it burn me all the way,
Down.

Lost inside my own head,
In our fantasy world,
Our limbs are entangled,
Covered in sweats.

''What do you think right now?,
You have this sly expression on your face?''
''Nothing particular,
Good thing, we did not even get started,
Yet.''

In The End

For all the times,
You stared down at me,
Thinking I was randomly drinking….

I was only celebrating
All my small victories
By myself.

Your ignorance
Only
Made
Me
Stronger
Than
Before.

Suck that now.

Survivor

You can always judge a book by its cover,
People by their scars.
I see how shallow you are,
If you were in my spot,
You would cower and cry.

That is why i smirk,
Hold a daring gaze
Every time
I catch people
Looking at my scars.

FALLing Back

I handed my heart out to fall,
The tide took it,
Cradled lovingly like a baby,
Carried it gently,
To the bottom.

Opening my arms wide,
My hair flying all over,
I throw myself over the edge.

I unite with my heart again,
The fall puts us together,
Stitches my heart back to the void,
Washes us away,
Away from eyes.

Shhhh, be quiet my heart,
Deep breaths, be still,
Here,
They will never find us.

Wet Kisses

Kiss me under the rain,
Let the rain
Wash away
All my insecurities.
Set me free.

Your heavy breathing,
The music of rain
The heavy drum of my own heart.

The whole world is silent
For a precious moment.
We fall into a bliss,
Wet kisses all over my face.

Prayers

''I gave you a nice home,
A stable car,
A job to pay your bills,
Hobbies to keep you occupied,
Skills to make things easier,
Still not satisfied???''

''Oh my God, seriously???
You gave me so many flaws,
Tried to balance them,
Messed it up,
Called it a game.
ARE YOU EVEN SERIOUS????''

Hush Hush Baby

You like it
When I am silent.
Then you can hear
The thoughts
Circling inside my head.

What you don't know
Can never hurt you
Or scar for a lifetime.

Hence The Irony

"How deep is your love?",
All these endless questions of yours.
I leaned in and whispered
To your lips,
"How deep can you dig a grave?''

Origami

Watching the amazement
Dance in your eyes
When you stare at
The origami hearts
I made for you.
Like my feelings,
I hang them up
To the heavy silence
Between us.

You watched the origami hearts
Sway gently with the breeze,
I watched you and the elephant in the room.

Winter Kiss

Always been a fan of snuggles in coach,
Kissing the hot chocolate from your lips.
Cracklings of the fire place,
Fire dancing on our skins-as if
Our passion is not hot enough.

A flannel blanket all over your naked skin,
My fingers tracing invisible patterns.
I devour what is left of the hot chocolate,
''Baby, it's smeared all over your skin.''

Popsicle hues of the northern lights,
Sparkling inside outside when you smile.
You had always been like Xmas lights,
I had always watched you in awe.

The white blanket under our feet,
The sound of our feet in the blissful silence,
-Crunch, crunch-
We walked together, hand in hand,
Created a path to the woods and back.

Loving All These Heartbreaks For Us   Cathy BLUE

We felt cold, warmed each other up
In the most delicious way.
Our skins glistening with the sweat,
You laid your head over my heart,
Led the slow beating of my heart
Lull you to asleep,
Until another round of
Love-making.

It kept snowing all night,
We drifted in and off of sleep.
I listened to your breathing,
I inhaled your scent all over my skin.

Ironic it is, how we take everything for granted,
Forgetting like seasons, everything has a time.

Biology Lessons

It is like a strip-tease, ya know?
I am doing a dance of seven veils,
Shedding my own skin,
Showing you what I am made of.

You stare at me and see all the flaws,
Comparing me in your mind with plastic Barbie dolls,
A little button nose here, a plump lip there,
What man would not want bigger breasts and hips?

I stare back to the mirror and get my veils back,
I leave my skin crumpled on the floor,
Wear steel armor instead.
Now, you can not penetrate my skin.

Journey To My Dreams

Restless and determined,
Chasing after something
I can never have.
Sad it is,
Knowing does not stop me,
Ironically adds more fuel
To the fire.

Never believed in
'When one door closes,
Another one opens' mantra.
Had to kick a lot of doors open.
May be I am one of these people,
Who can't take no for an answer.

A perfectionist is the polite synonym
For a control freak,
Never been a fan of perfunctory,
World needs more perfectionists.

Running wild, I broke my chains.
Untamed, wild with energy.

They see me running,
I feel their judgemental glares on my back.

Words lift me in the air,
Everything else blurs,
The pull is too strong,
I don’t have the heart in me
To resist.

May be not tomorrow,
Mark my words,
When I get there,
You will not like
To see,
What my signature reads
On your signed book.

Coffee Heaven

''Opps, sorry,'' you apologise,
Noticing you accidently drank from my cup.
I shrug and take back my cup
From your hands,
''No biggie,'' i reply,
Acting all nonchalant.

Now, your mouth tastes like heaven.
Babe, I can get addicted with a kiss.

Toxic Family

Watching you trying to dig and dig,
In a funny attempt to remove the ivy
From your *-oh-so-perfect*ly tended garden.
I smirk, cue the irony.

Every poison in life,
They have their roots
Buried deep.

The Last Chapter

You are now an archive of old poems,
The words stayed on the pale paper,
Feelings? Long dead...

Me Versus Them

I had made so many mistakes,
Some of them, I can't shake.

Life has never been a piece of cake,
Most of it had been *'smile and fake'*.

Forced by the polite rules of society to partake,
There had always been too much at stake.

I plead for a brake,
There is too much I can't take.

Please throw me in a lake,
That will be best for your own sake.

I'm in my late-wake,
For peace, I ache.

I'm unique like a snowflake,
All this uniqueness, society forces you to rake...

Motherhood

I had seen so many shit,
Left me too damaged
Like a sinking ship.
You were right,
With the damage I took,
I can never be
A home
For a lover.

I got two miracles
Who look up at me
Like I am the life itself,
So in awe and in love.
I am not just a mother,
I am a home to them,
To my own childhood as well.

Trying my best
To fix what they broke
Without any care.
I am gonna break
The f*king circle.

New Motto

Chin up girl,
Grow and glow.
You know how
They hate,
When you show,
Who is way down below.
Put up a good show!

First Childhood Memory You Remember

You towered over mum,
Holding a knife to her neck,
Screaming to her face,
Knowing she is stuck
Between you and the kitchen counter,
Nowhere to run.

I was a child, I cried for help.
Nobody helped.
I was a child, I blinked my tears,
I grew up.

Worthless

I asked for a flicker of love,
You refused to give.
I lit a candle, burnt the bridge down.
I won't beg for a piece of love.

My Scales

Life has never given me lemons.
I was given an endless fury.
I shaped it, morphed it into scales.
Now, I'm the dragon
They all tell tales about me,
Fearing to be unleashed.

Heartfelt

There had always been differences
With what you said / How you acted.

Belittling me inside my cage,
Flattering me outside my cage
('Cos we had audience,
I know how much you like to perform,
Definitely Oscar winning material!!!!)

Unaware of what your future holds,
I keep everything to myself,
I saw the hand I was dealt,
I got the Queen and 2 Aces.

Ironic, now your words will fall
On my deaf ears,
For once, I will be blind, deaf and muted.
Sorry means nothing now,
I am rising from my ashes.

''You may wanna fall back now.''

Cruel Queen

I had been there many times,
The rock bottom, you know,
The lowest of low.
I answered the questions:
How deep can you sink?
How long can you get?

I had always been a survivor,
A wounded warrior, a restless fighter,
A fallen to some,
A Cruel Queen to all.

Now, sitting on my throne,
I am looking down to y'all,
Laughing my ass off.

Crying Myself To Sleep

They all think,
I am depressed.
After all their lies,
Small manipulations here and there,
I just stopped caring.

I lay down in the bed,
Everything feels claustrophobic,
The air I tend to breathe,
The body I try to fit in.

My sky catches fire,
Everywhere is covered with smoke.
'HELP!' I want to scream out of my lungs.

I will cry myself to sleep tonight...

Self-Care

Dark thoughts of gray,
Rained all over me.
I got caught unprepared,
I got soaked till my bones.
I got cold,
I got sick.

I came home,
Made myself a cup of tea.
''I will always take care of you, baby,'',
I lulled myself to sleep.

Hope

When you ask me how much I love you or
What I would do to prove my love for you…

Babe, I've been savouring all the poisonous words,
Coming out of your mouth,
Hoping to prove my worth.

Hope is the 3 monkeys: blind, deaf, mute.
My heart and brain, always in dispute.

Farewell

I had bottled up too much,
This time.
Couldn't breathe,
Didn't feel like livin'.
So I cried,
I wrote everything down.
Deaf ears, blind eyes.
Mute papers held
All my silent screams,
Heart breaks,
Pain and all my heart.

-He tried to give me a sweet release,
I had always found it
In the comfort of my own words,
My hard-won solace.-

Every end is a new beginning,
These words built up a forte for me,
Kept me safe in a cocoon,
I will be a heartbreakingly beautiful
Butterfly in my new era.

www.ingramcontent.com/pod-product-compliance
Lightning Source LLC
LaVergne TN
LVHW091117150826
845673LV00002B/871

9786250098165